HOW TO TEACH YOUR CHILDREN ABOUT GOD...

Without Actually Scaring Them Out of Their Wits

BOOKS BY THE BERENSTAINS

How to Teach Your Children About God
    Without Actually Scaring Them Out of Their Wits
How to Teach Your Children About Sex
    Without Making a Complete Fool of Yourself
It's All in the Family
It's Still in the Family
Berenstains' Baby Book
Baby Makes Four
Marital Blitz
Lover Boy
Bedside Lover Boy
I Love You Kid, But Oh My Wife
Office Lover Boy
Have a Baby, My Wife Just Had a Cigar
What Dr. Freud Didn't Tell You
Flipsville-Squaresville
Mr. Dirty vs. Mrs. Clean
You Could Diet Laughing
Education: Impossible
Never Trust Anyone Over 13
Are Parents for Real?
Be Good or I'll Belt Ya

CHILDREN'S BOOKS

The Big Honey Hunt
The Bike Lesson
The Bears' Picnic
The Bear Scouts
The Bears' Vacation
The Bears' Christmas
Inside Outside Upside Down
Bears on Wheels
Old Hat, New Hat
Bears in the Night
Berenstains' B Book

HOW TO TEACH YOUR CHILDREN ABOUT GOD...

Without Actually Scaring Them Out of Their Wits

MOMMY! DADDY! SOMETHING'S HAPPENED TO BUSTER! HE'S ROLLED OVER ON HIS BACK AND HIS EYES ARE LIKE LITTLE "X"s!

by Stan and Jan Berenstain

The McCall Publishing Company   **New York**

Copyright © 1971 by Stanley and Janice Berenstain

All rights reserved. No part of this work may be reproduced or transmitted in any form or by any means, electronic or mechanical, including photocopy, recording, or any information storage and retrieval system, without permission in writing from the publisher.

Published simultaneously in Canada by Doubleday Canada Ltd., Toronto

Library of Congress Catalog Card Number 76-154244

ISBN 0-8415-0114-9

The McCall Publishing Company
230 Park Avenue
New York, New York 10017

Printed in the United States of America

Sooner...

— OR LATER,

BLAM

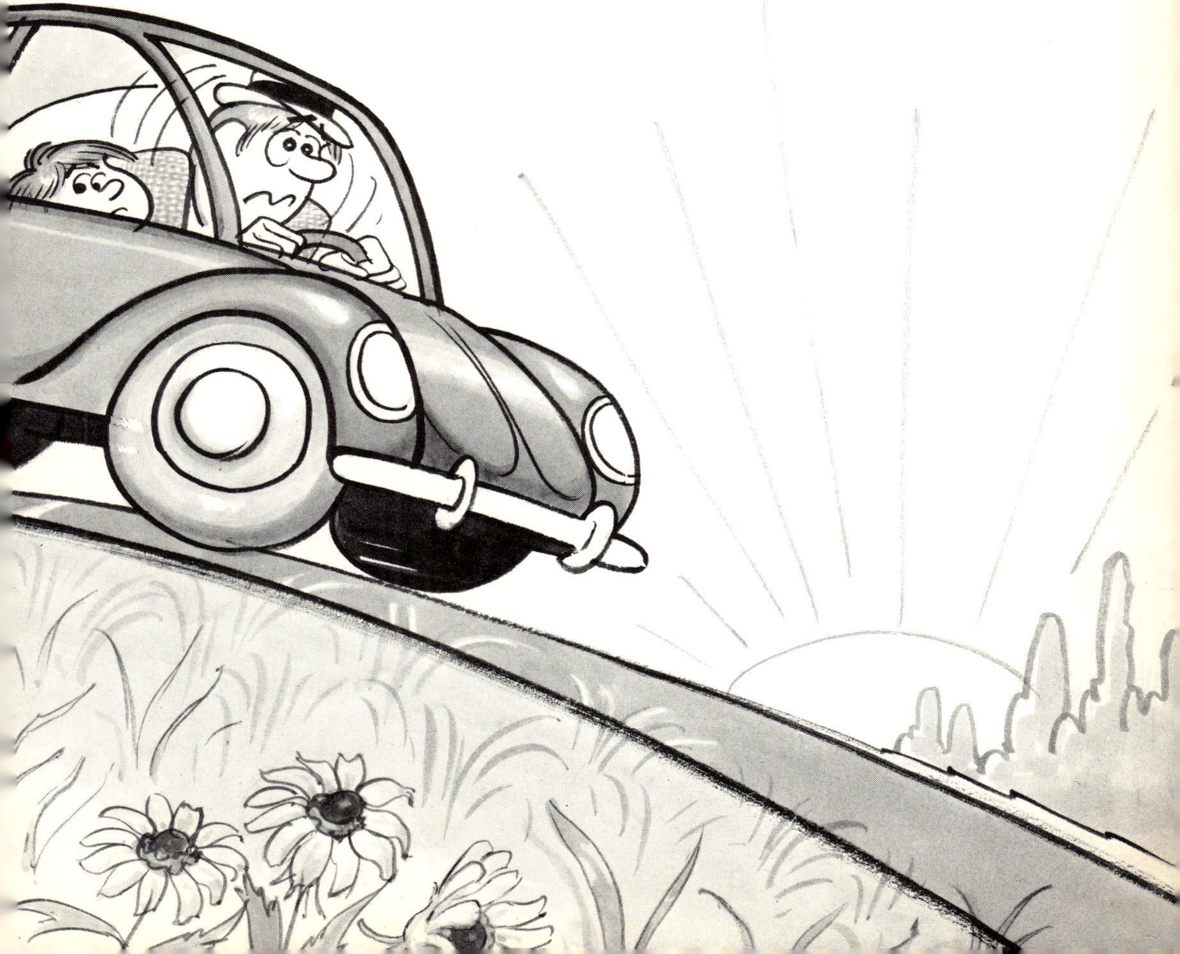

— IN THE NORMAL COURSE OF EVENTS,

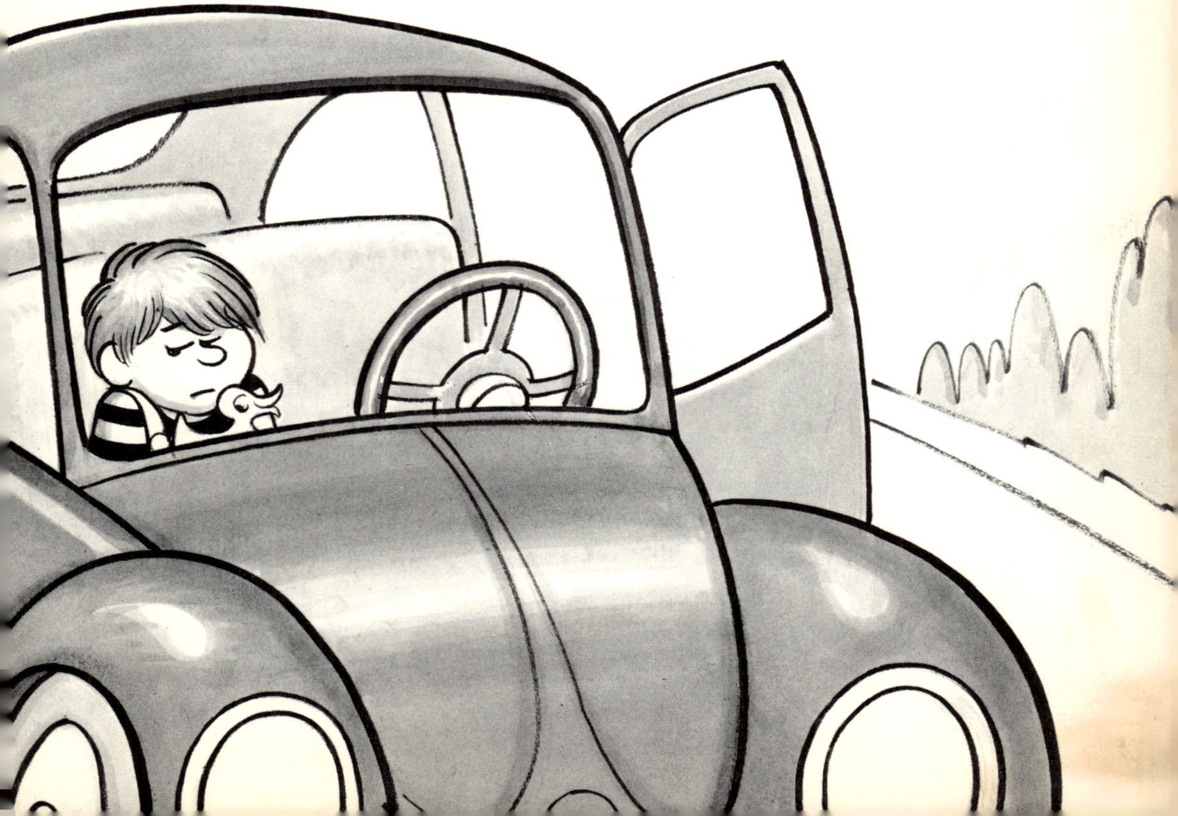

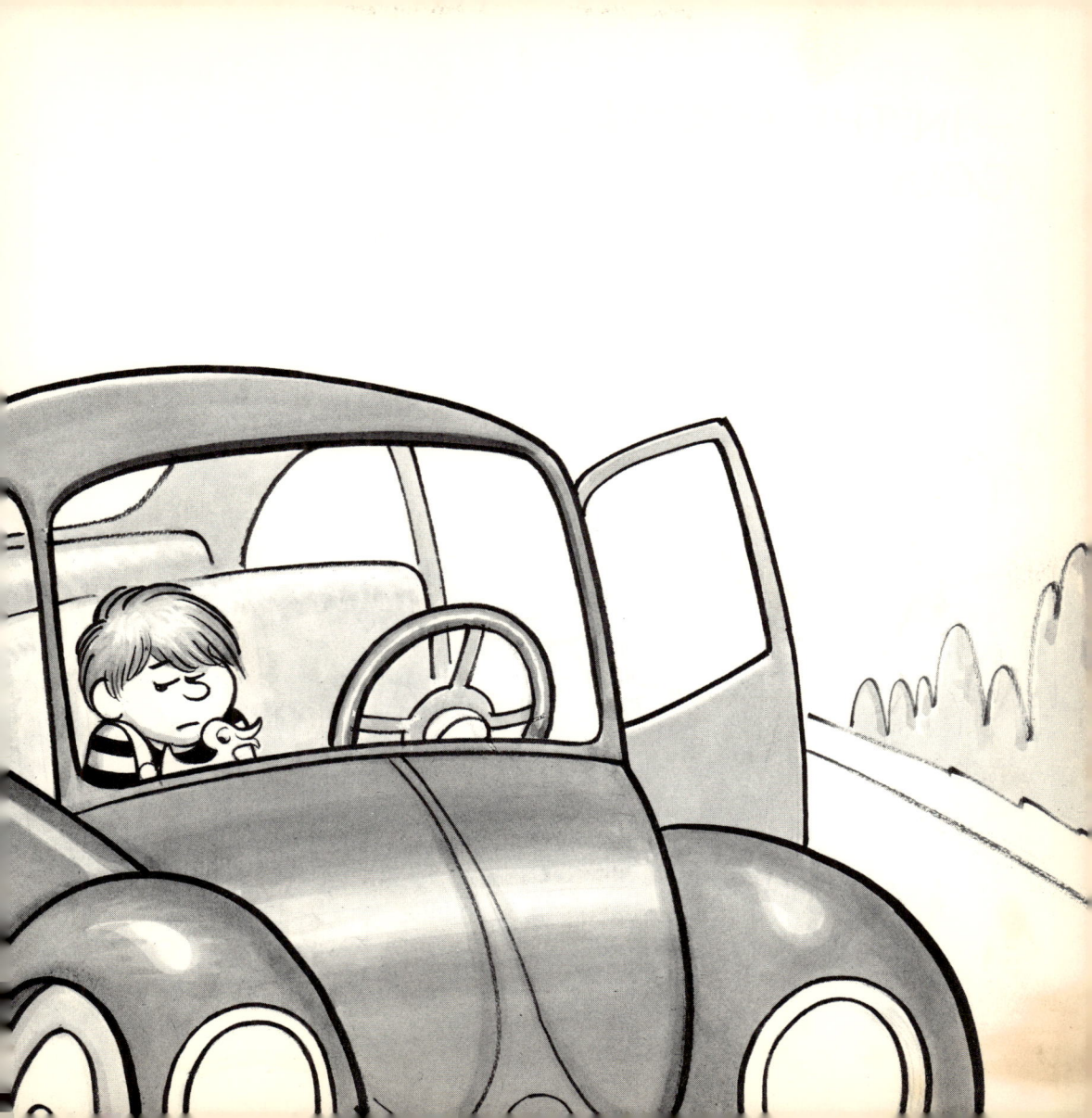

—THE QUESTION IS GOING TO COME UP...

DADDY...

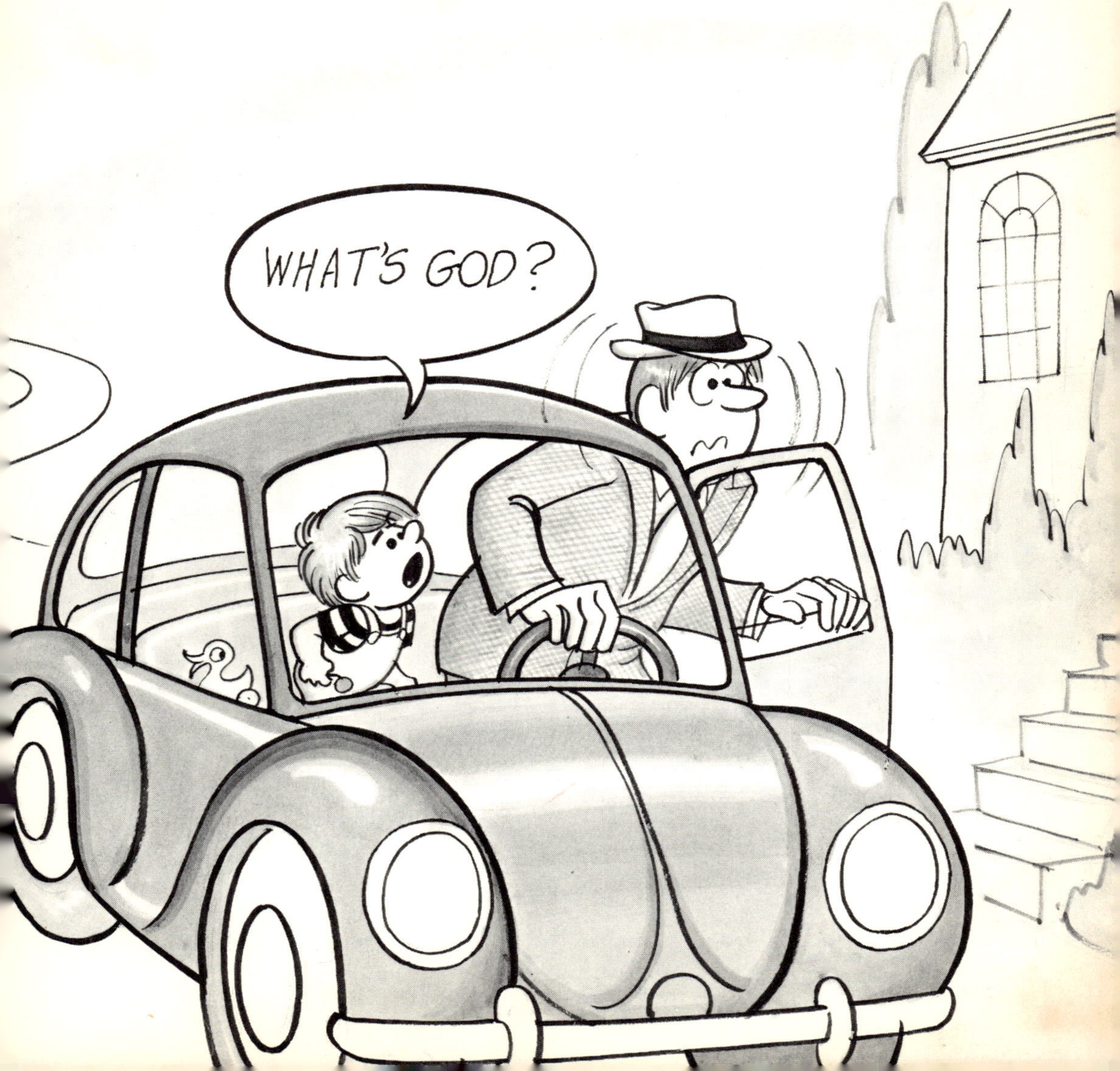
WHAT'S GOD?

THERE'S JUST NO GETTING AWAY FROM IT . . .

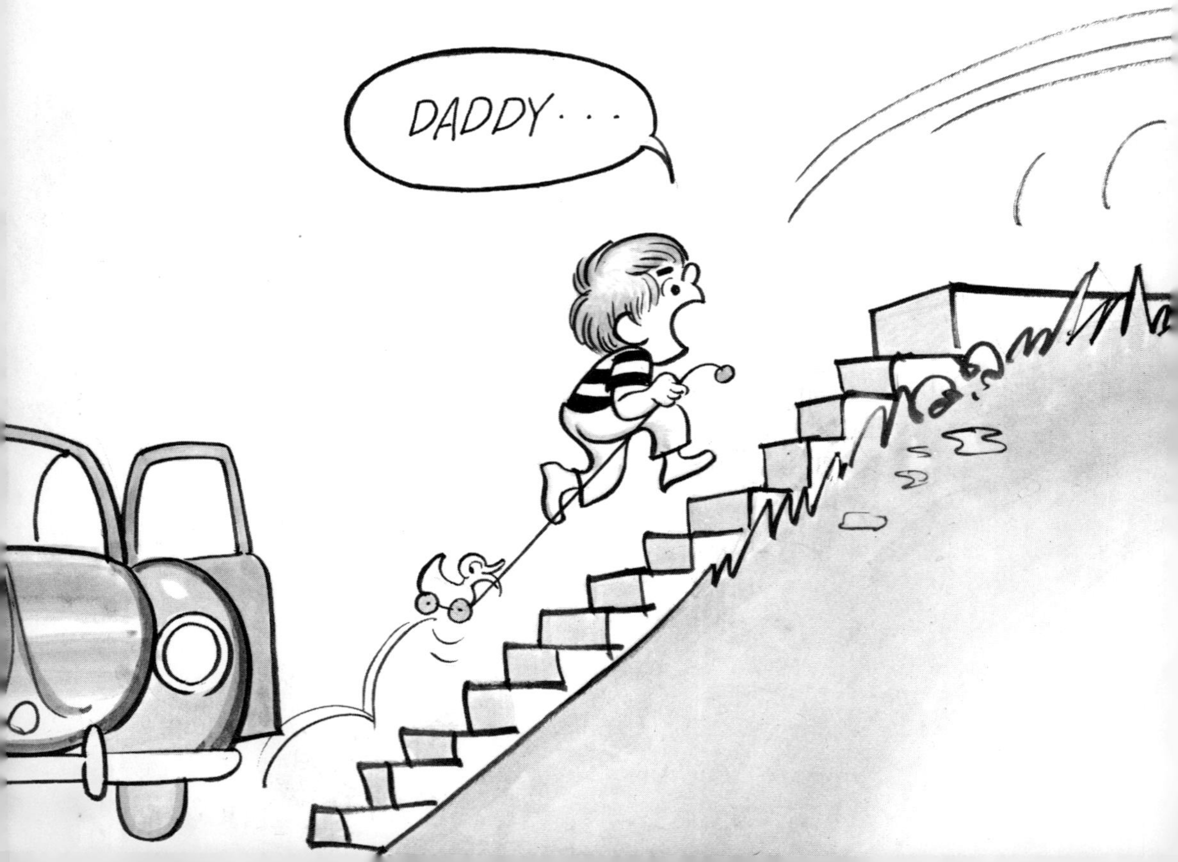

—EVENTUALLY YOU ARE GOING TO HAVE TO TELL YOUR YOUNGSTER ABOUT · · ·

Him

SOME PARENTS, ON THE THEORY THAT YOU DON'T FOOL AROUND WITH THE MAN UPSTAIRS, TAKE NO CHANCES...

— AND SOCK JUNIOR INTO SUNDAY SCHOOL SO FAST HIS LITTLE HEAD SPINS!

But, Honey, this is a synagogue!
So?
But we're not even Jewish!
Shh! They'll hear you!

MOST PARENTS, HOWEVER, UNDERSTAND THAT THEY ARE RESPONSIBLE FOR THEIR CHILD'S SPIRITUAL AS WELL AS HIS PHYSICAL AND EMOTIONAL WELL-BEING AND MEET THE GOD QUESTION HEAD-ON.

"Son, I'm glad you asked me that question—"

THOSE OF A PHILOSOPHICAL TURN OF MIND...

"It happens to be a question that people have been asking for a _very long_ time..."

—HAVING GIVEN THE SUBJECT OF GOD AND HIS CREATION CONSIDERABLE THOUGHT, DISCHARGE THEIR RESPONSIBILITY AS JUNIOR'S FIRST TEACHER...

— BY BORING JUNIOR PRACTICALLY OUT OF

HIS SKULL

LIONS AND
STARS AND PLANETS - BLAH
-- BLAH-BLAH--EACH--BLAH-
OWN APPOINTED
TIME AND PLACE-- BLA
STRETCHED TO INF
BLAH-

OTHER PARENTS, NOT HAVING GIVEN THE SUBJECT ANY THOUGHT AT ALL, HAVE NO SUCH DIFFICULTY.

THEY KNOW INTUITIVELY THAT A CONFIDENT ASSURANCE OF GOD'S LOVE...

– UNDERLINED BY A SIMPLE CHILD'S PRAYER...

If I should die before I wake I pray the Lord my SOUL TO TAKE
-IS ALL THAT IS NEEDED . . .

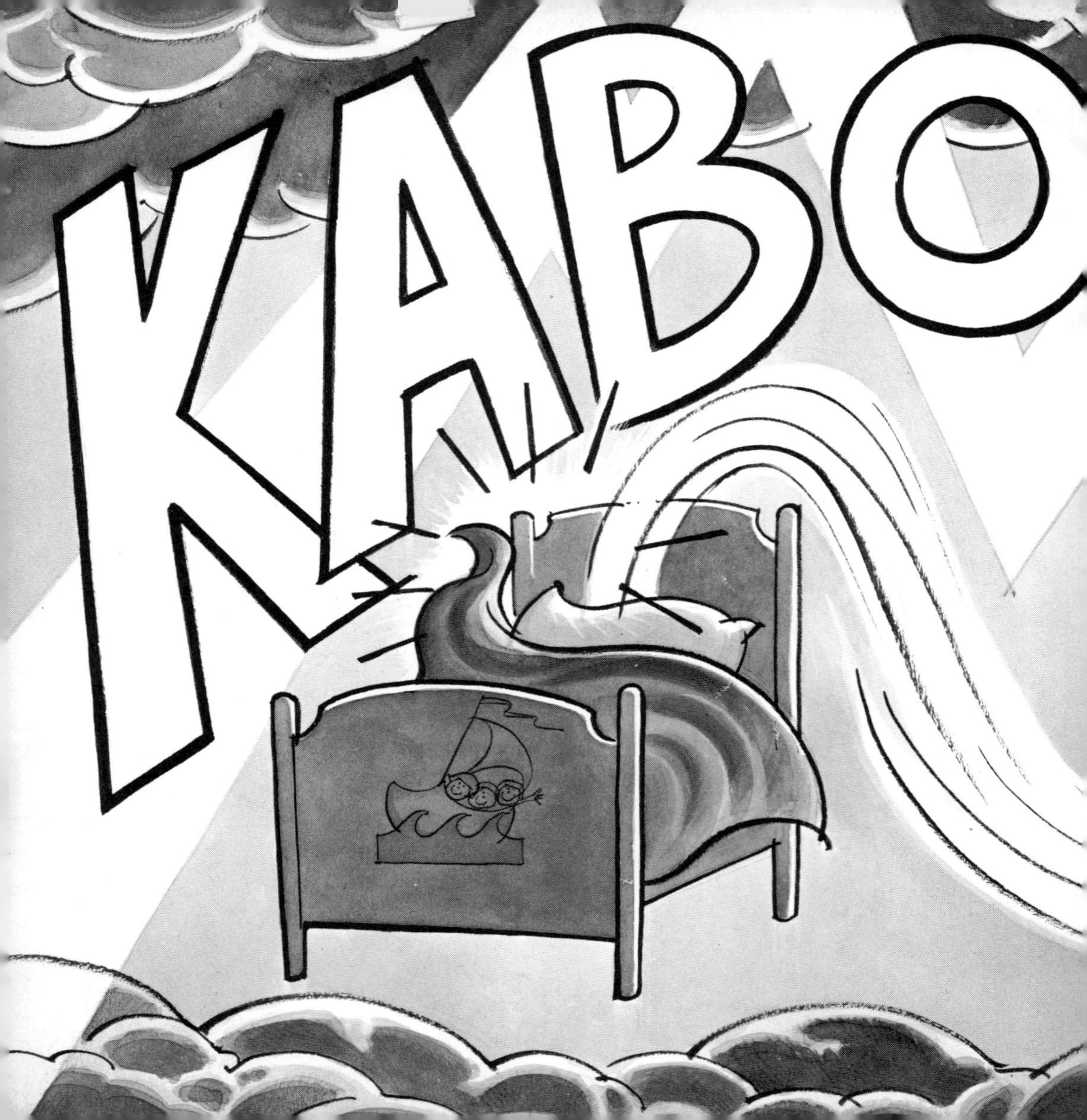
KABO

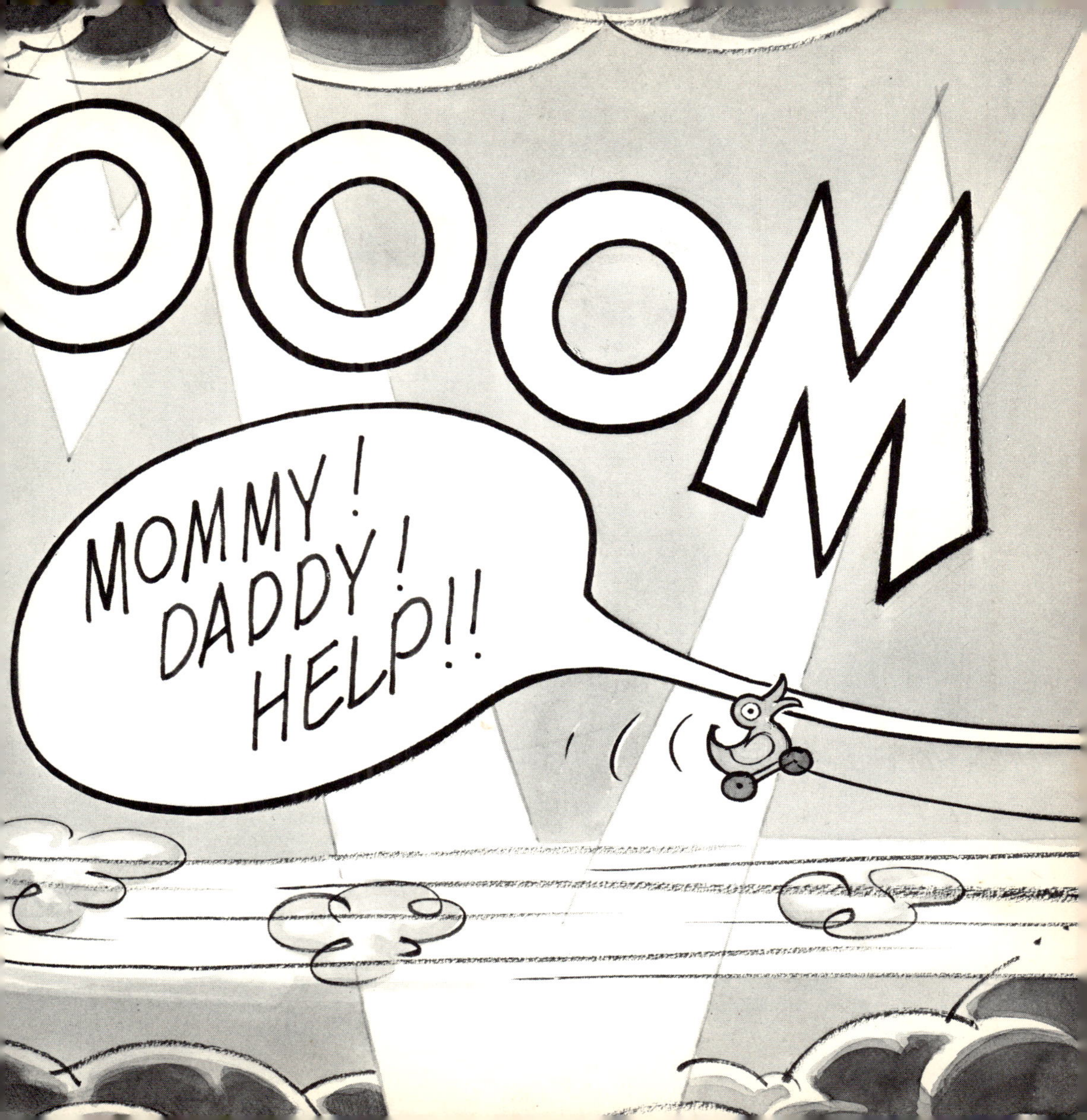
OOOOM
MOMMY! DADDY! HELP!!

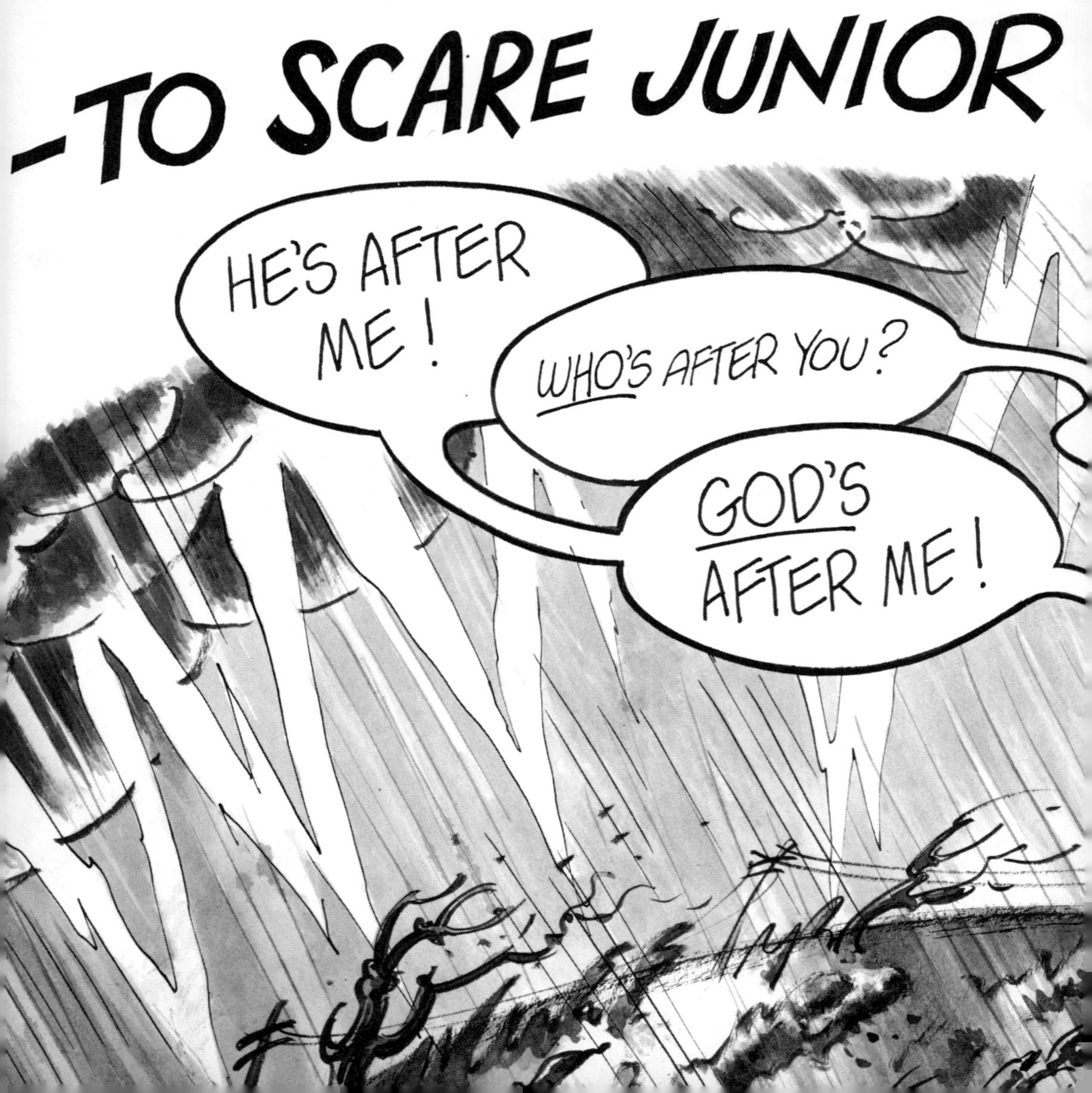

-TO SCARE JUNIOR
HE'S AFTER ME!
WHO'S AFTER YOU?
GOD'S AFTER ME!

PRACTICALLY OUT OF HIS WITS!

BUT, SWEETIE, GOD LOVES YOU VERY MUCH!

Yeah... then how come he's after me?

But most parents manage to steer a middle course between the remote God of the universe and that fearsome fellow who is so ready your soul to take if you should die before you wake, and find a way to tell Junior about God in terms he can understand and relate to ···

. . . the rain, the sunshine, the rainbow - they're all God's work, Son - all part of God's Great Plan - -

—AND EVEN ESTABLISH A MEANINGFUL SEARCHING DIALOGUE ON THE SUBJECT . . .

Did he make trees?
Of course!
and flowers?
Absolutely!
and butterflies?
EVERYTHING!

Did he make worms?
soup?
spiders?
teeth?
school?
asparagus?
vultures?
NOW, LOOK . . . I TOLD YOU . . . IT'S ALL PART OF GOD'S GREAT PLAN!

BELLY ACHES?
MEASLES?
POLLUTION?
EARTHQUAKES?
TORNADOES?
FLOODS?
HIPPIES?

AND THEN SOCK HIM
INTO SUNDAY SCHOOL
SO FAST HIS
LITTLE HEAD SPINS
WAR?
H-BOMBS?
NAPALM?

Today, boys and girls, we are going to hear the wonderful story of Noah and the Ark . . .
MOSQUITOES.?
EGGPLANT?
SPLINTERS?

SUNDAY SCHOOL IS NO LONGER THE CLOSED, HANDS-FOLDED EXPERIENCE IT ONCE WAS. MODERN RELIGIOUS EDUCATORS HAVE RECOGNIZED THE VALUE OF MANY OF THE IDEAS AND PRACTICES OF SECULAR EDUCATION AND HAVE OPENED THEIR INSTITUTIONS TO SUCH TOOLS AND TECHNIQUES AS...

— VISUAL AIDS

-LA-DE DAH...

"OH, MY DOODNETH! HERE COME A <u>BIG</u> THNAKE!"

- SHOW AND TELL
When you pull the string, Praying Mandy says her prayers...
- FIELD TRIPS
THE PROPHET OF THE LORD
IT'S X RATED!
-AND, OF COURSE, THE P.T.A.
I DON'T BELIEVE I'VE SEEN YOU FOLKS AT REGULAR SUNDAY SERVICES

THE BIBLE, OF COURSE, REMAINS THE FOUNDATION OF RELIGIOUS EDUCATION. INDEED, THE RELEVANCE OF BIBLICAL STORIES TO EVERYDAY BEHAVIOR IS OFTEN QUITE STARTLING. AN ALERT SUNDAY SCHOOL TEACHER, FOR EXAMPLE, NEEDN'T LOOK MUCH FURTHER THAN THE END OF HER NOSE TO FIND · · ·

DAVID AND GOLIATH,

THE TOWER OF BABEL.

JOSEPH AND THE COAT OF MANY COLORS,

PESTILENCE,

SODOM AND GOMORRAH,

—AND ALL MANNER OF FLOODS AND NATURAL DISASTERS.

CHILDREN ARE ENCOURAGED TO EXPRESS THEMSELVES IN THE MODERN SUNDAY SCHOOL — TO EXPLORE FOR THEMSELVES THE MEANINGS AND VALUES INHERENT IN THE GREAT TEACHINGS.

Our Pictures About Noah

THE HAPPY ENDING IS A POPULAR THEME WITH MANY CHILDREN.

Noah and all the Animals landed on Mt. Arrowroot and Lived Happy ever After — Mt Arrowroot

A FEW KIDS IDENTIFY WITH THE UNDERDOG.

THE VAST MAJORITY, HOWEVER, ROOT FOR THE YANKEES.

THE CHILD WHO ALWAYS PUTS AERIAL DOGFIGHTS IN HIS PICTURES PRESENTS A SPECIAL PROBLEM...

—AS DOES THE YOUNGSTER WHO SEES THE STORY OF NOAH IN A SOMEWHAT NARROW, BUT NONETHELESS VALID, PERSPECTIVE...

— NOT TO MENTION THE CLASS SMARTASS...

> HEER LIES NOAH
> IF NOAh WAS 950 Yrs OLD hee WOOD Be **DED**

— AND THE CHILD WHO ALWAYS SPOILS HIS DRAWINGS AND WADS THEM UP AND THROWS THEM AT PEOPLE.

BUT, MOST REWARDING TO A SUNDAY SCHOOL TEACHER IS <u>THAT RARE CHILD WHO REALLY GETS THE MESSAGE</u> AND SEES CLEARLY THE APPLICATION OF THE GREAT BIBLE STORIES TO OUR LIVES TODAY.

"WHERE ARE YOU GOING?"

"LOOKS LIKE RAIN — I'M GOING HOME AND START BUILDING A BOAT!"

"..300 CUBITS LONG BY 50 CUBITS WIDE.."

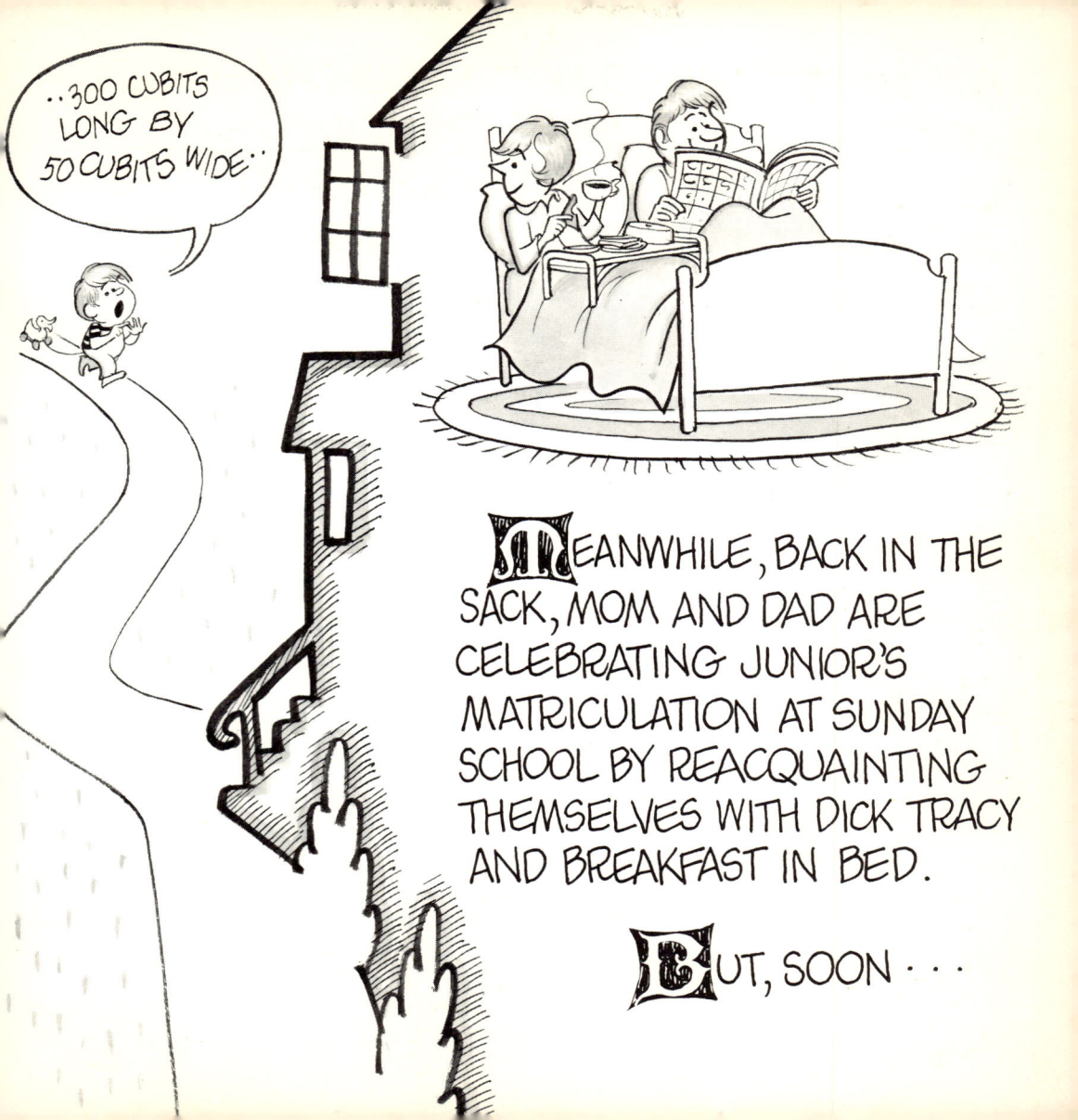

MEANWHILE, BACK IN THE SACK, MOM AND DAD ARE CELEBRATING JUNIOR'S MATRICULATION AT SUNDAY SCHOOL BY REACQUAINTING THEMSELVES WITH DICK TRACY AND BREAKFAST IN BED.

BUT, SOON · · ·

–PERHAPS THROUGH THE MYSTERIOUS WORKINGS OF CONSCIENCE . . .
. . . and God said unto Noah: Make thee an ark of gopher wood, and pitch it within and without with pitch
That's nice - and what else did you learn in Sunday School?

– PERHAPS THROUGH DIALOGUE WITH THEIR LITTLE SUNDAY SCHOOLER,
WE LEARNED THAT EVERY KID WHOSE PARENTS COME TO SERVICES EVERY WEEK UNTIL EASTER GETS A CHOCOLATE BUNNY!
– FALLEN-AWAY PARENTS FIND THEMSELVES BEING INEXORABLY, IRRESISTIBLY DRAWN . . .

—BACK INTO THE RELIGIOUS COMMUNITY.

♪ ROCK-OF-AGES--- ♫

WHETHER THIS EXPERIENCE PROVES TO BE JUST ANOTHER EPISODE IN THE ODYSSEY OF PARENTHOOD, LIKE LITTLE LEAGUE OR DANCE CLASS..

—OR A GENUINE RENEWAL OF FAITH . . .

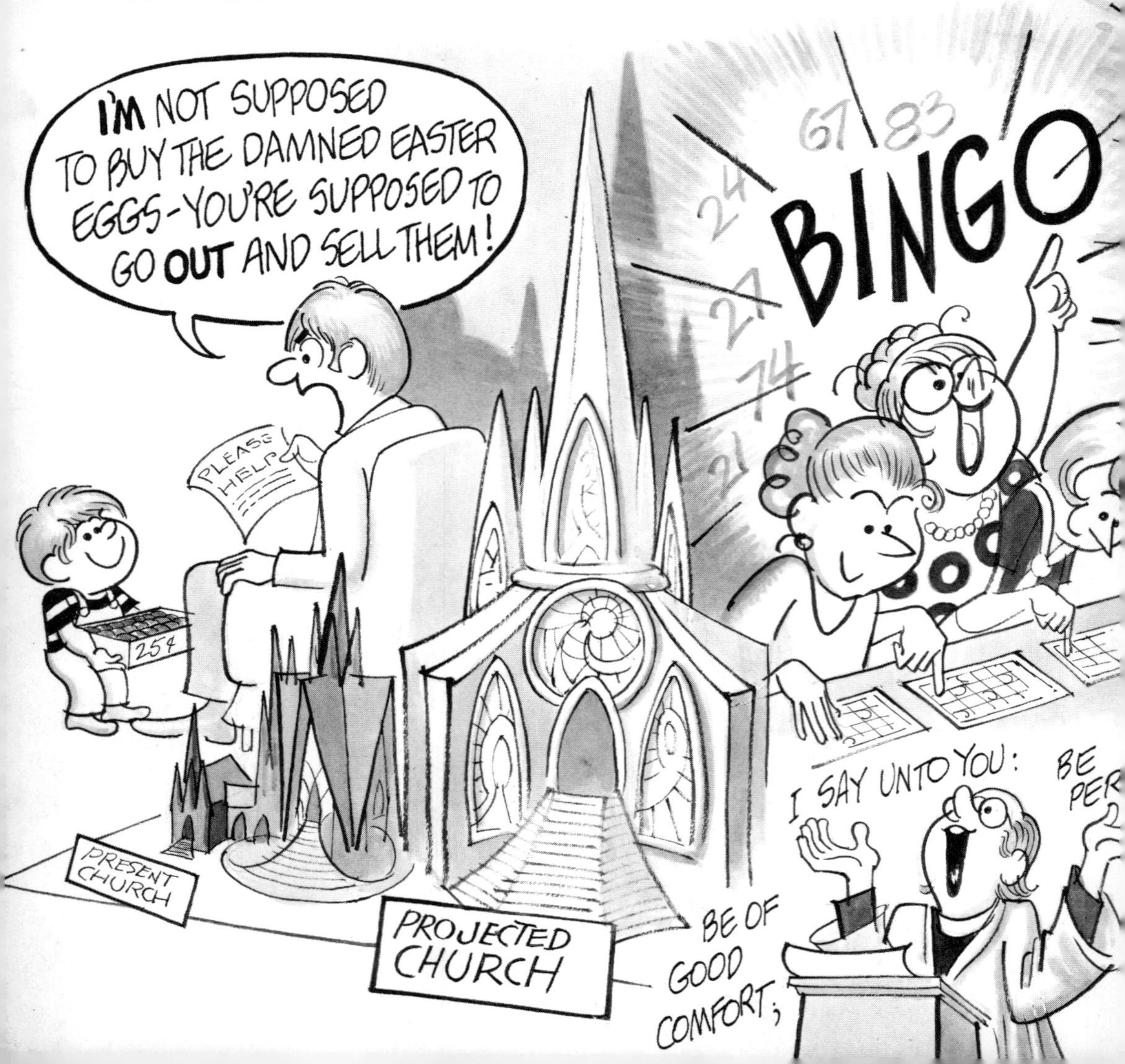

—DEPENDS LARGELY ON THE NATURE OF THE EXPERIENCE.

WHILE PARENTS ARE ENTITLED TO ALL THE HELP THEY CAN GET IN ANSWERING THEIR CHILDREN'S QUESTIONS ABOUT GOD, THERE ARE SOME EXPERIENCES WHICH ARE SO HIGHLY CHARGED THAT THEY SHOULD BE DEALT WITH ONLY IN THE BOSOM OF THE FAMILY — SUCH EXPERIENCES, FOR EXAMPLE, AS THE DEATH OF A LOVED ONE ···

BUSTER!

"MOMMY! DADDY! SOMETHING'S HAPPENED TO BUSTER! HE'S ROLLED OVER ON HIS BACK AND HIS EYES ARE LIKE LITTLE "X"S!"

IT IS A GREAT TEMPTATION AT TIMES LIKE THESE TO TRY TO PROTECT JUNIOR...

– TO SHIELD HIM FROM THE FACTS,

-BUT IT IS A TEMPTATION TO BE RESISTED. FOR ONE THING, YOU ARE UNLIKELY TO GET AWAY WITH IT . . .
PET SHOP
That's not Buster. Buster had a freckle on his tail and a speckle on his belly.

—BUT MORE IMPORTANT, JUNIOR IS ENTITLED TO GRIEVE FOR HIS LOST FRIEND,

—TO COMMEMORATE THE LOSS WITH A MODEST BUT DIGNIFIED FUNERAL...

—AND TO BEGIN THE LONG QUESTIONING JOURNEY OF THOUGHT ABOUT LIFE AND DEATH, GOD AND LITTLE FISH···

DADDY?

YES, SON

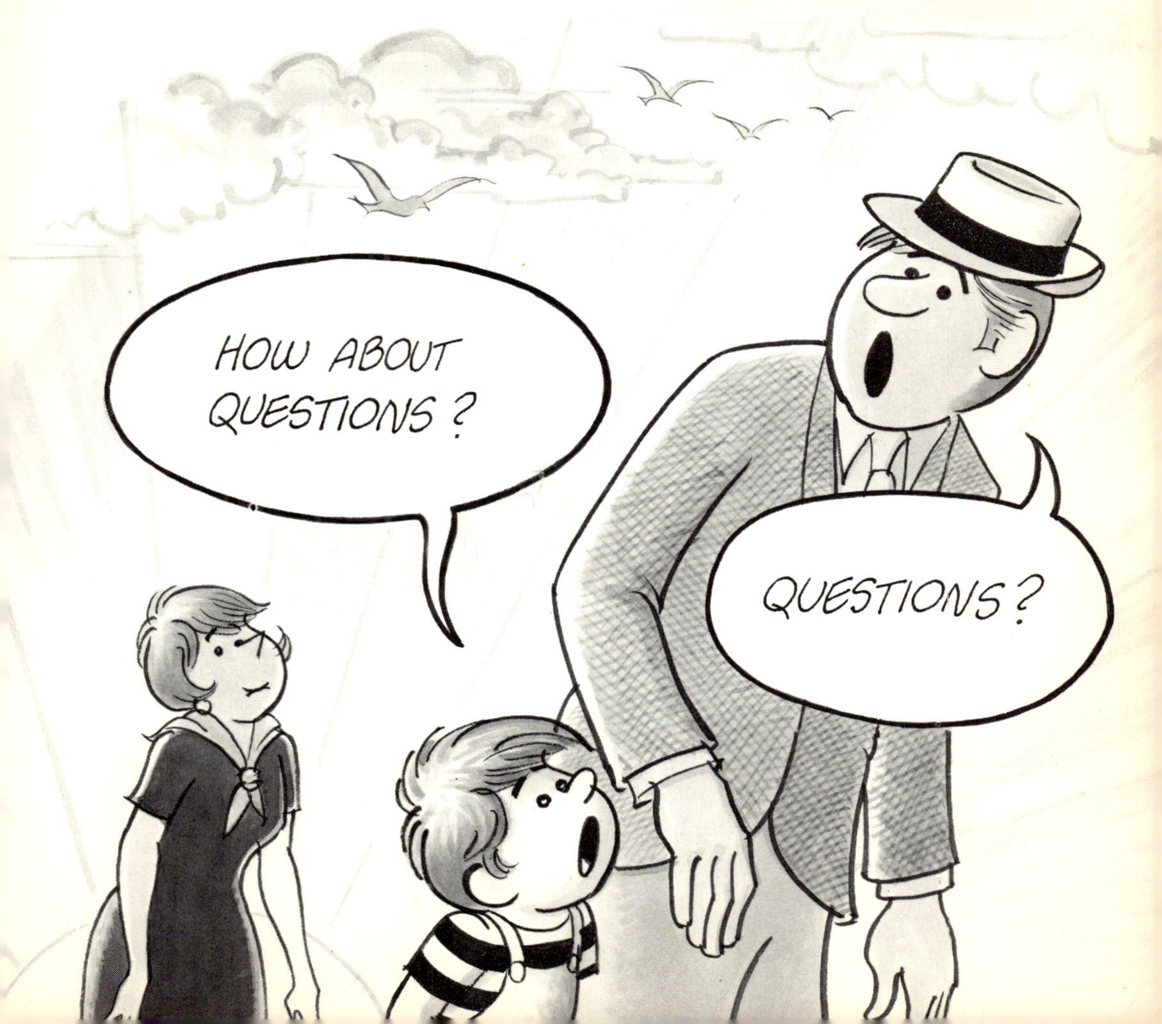
HOW ABOUT QUESTIONS?
QUESTIONS?

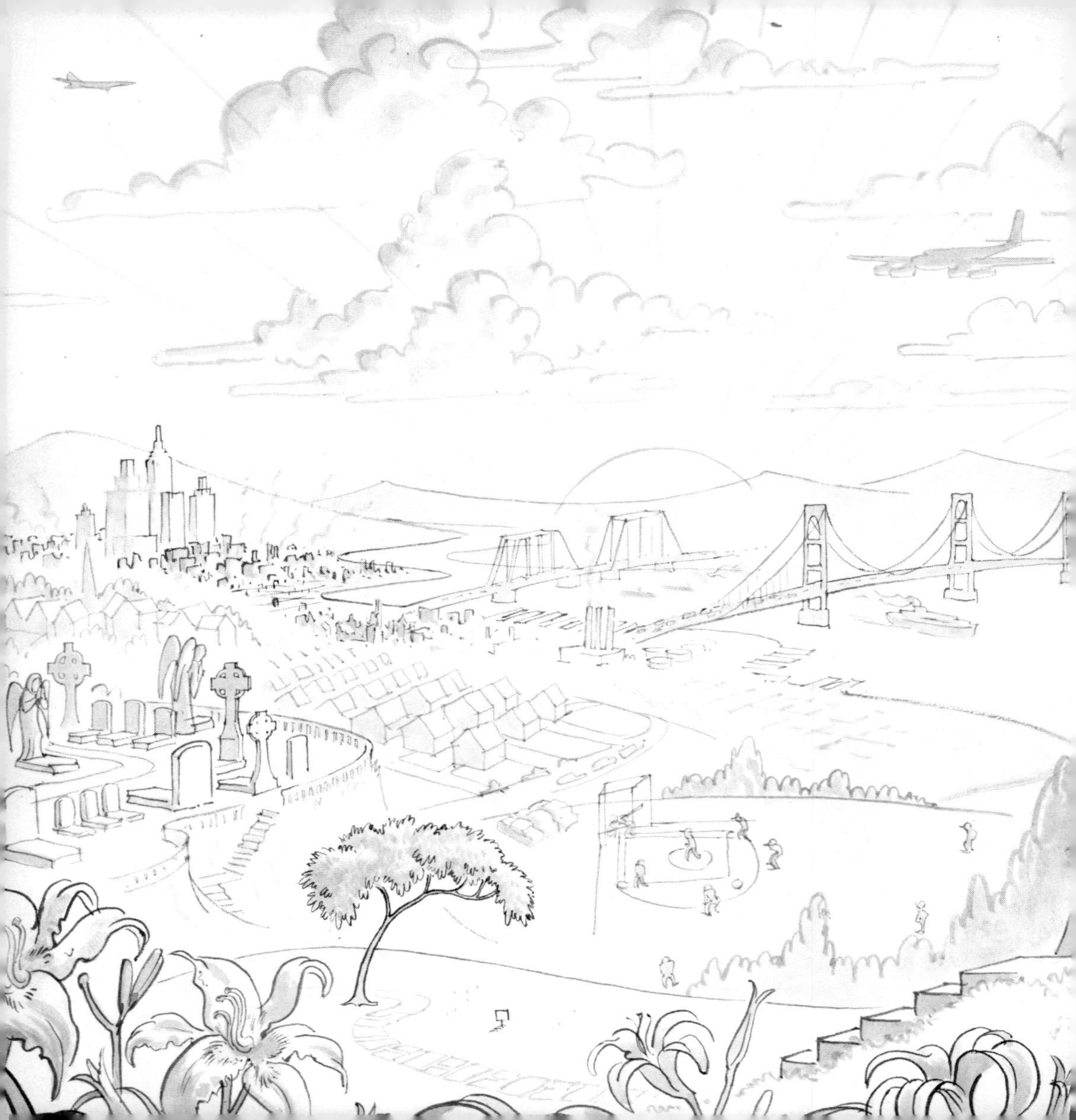

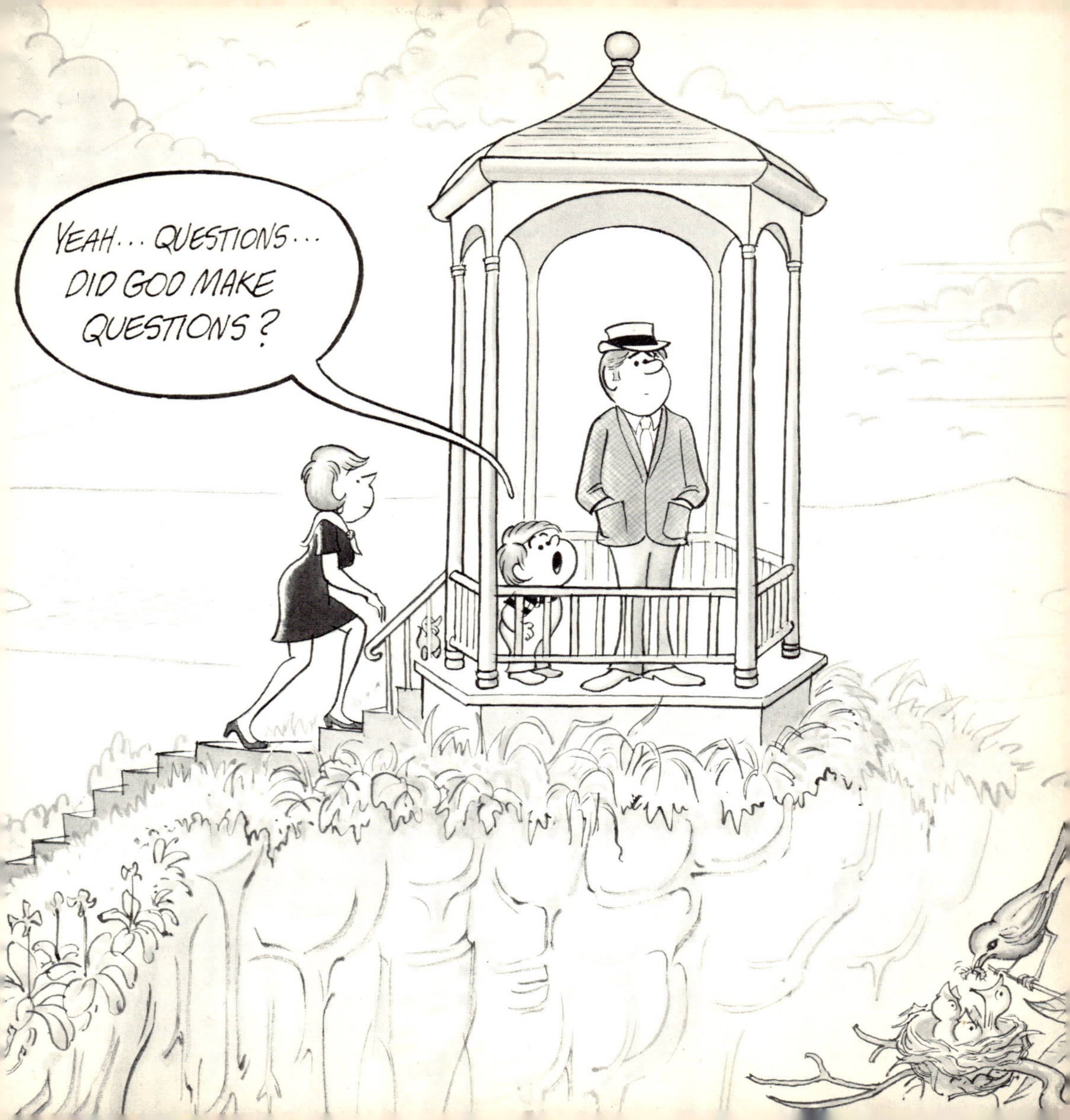
YEAH... QUESTIONS... DID GOD MAKE QUESTIONS?

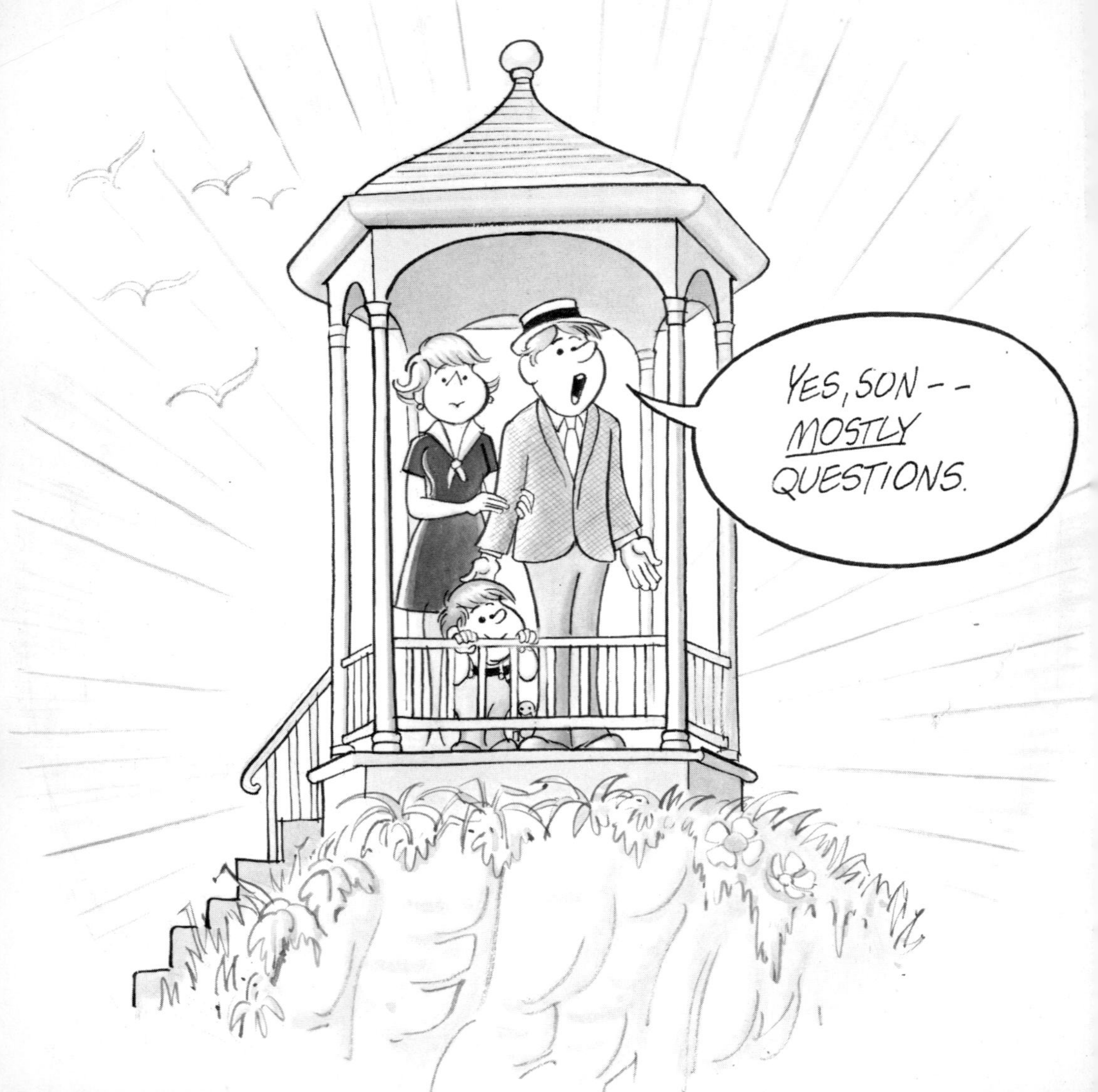
YES, SON--
MOSTLY
QUESTIONS.